Walt

Disney

Walt Disney

Creator of Magical Worlds

by
Charnan
Simon

Children's Press®
A Division of Grolier Publishing
New York / London / Hong Kong / Sydney
Danbury, Connecticut

Photo Credits

This book makes reference to various Disney copyrighted characters, trademarks, marks and registered marks owned by Disney Enterprises, Inc., and are used by permission from Disney Enterprises, Inc.

Cover: *Mr. Walt Disney*, © Disney Enterprises, Inc./Brown Brothers.

Back cover: *Sleeping Beauty Castle at DISNEYLAND PARK®*, ©Disney Enterprises, Inc./Stock Boston: (Michele Burgess).

The following photographs copyright © Disney Enterprises, Inc. and: AP/Wide World Photos: 17, 18 top, 24, 30; Archive Photos: 2, 12, 14, 35, 39; Brown Brothers: 3, 6 (RKO Pictures), 34; Corbis-Bettmann: 40 (UPI), 26 (UPI/Oscar Statuette© A.M.P.A.S®); Disney Enterprises, Inc.: 8, 9, 15, 21, 32; Globe Photos: 23; H. Armstrong Roberts, Inc.: 41 (J. Messerschmidt); Kobal Collection: 28 top; Photofest: 7, 28 bottom; Superstock, Inc.: 10, 42.

Additional photographs copyright ©: Corbis-Bettmann: 18 bottom; H. Armstrong Roberts, Inc.: 44 (R. Walker), 25 (Schwertner/Zefa), 36; Tony Stone Images: 45 (Rossanne Olson).

Reading Consultant
Linda Cornwell, Coordinator of School Quality and Professional Improvement, Indiana State Teachers Association

Visit Children's Press on the Internet at:
http://publishing.grolier.com

Library of Congress Cataloging-in-Publication Data
Simon, Charnan.
    Walt Disney : creator of magical worlds / by Charnan Simon.
        p. cm. — (Community builders)
    Includes bibliographical references and index.
    Summary: A biography of the animation pioneer who created Mickey Mouse and other popular characters and founded Disney Studios.
    ISBN: 0-516-21198-6 (lib. bdg.) 0-516-26515-6 (pbk.)
    1. Disney, Walt, 1901–1966—Juvenile literature. 2. Animators—United States—Biography—Juvenile literature. [1. Disney, Walt, 1901–1966. 2. Motion pictures—Biography.] I. Title. II. Series.
NC1766.U52D562 1999
791.43'092—dc21
[B]
           98-46686
           CIP
           AC

GROLIER
PUBLISHING
  2 3 4 5 6 7 8 9 10 R 08 07 06 05 04 03 02 01 00

Contents

This photograph of Walt Disney was taken in 1944.

Making Dreams Come True

Mickey Mouse. Donald Duck. Goofy and Pluto. Was there ever a time in your life when you didn't know these characters? Do you know anyone who doesn't recognize their names and faces?

Mickey, Donald, Goofy, and Pluto are all the cartoon inventions of Walt Disney. Mickey was created in 1928. Donald Duck, Goofy (who started out as Dippy Dawg), and

Mickey Mouse, Goofy, Donald Duck, and Pluto sing carols in a scene from "A Disney Channel Christmas."

7

Pluto followed soon after. With these and other cartoon characters, Walt Disney pioneered the art of animated film cartoons.

Animation

These four animated cartoons (from left to right) illustrate the way Mickey Mouse can "jump" across the ocean on a globe from one continent to another.

In live-action movies, filmmakers record the real, live actions of real, live actors. Animation is different. An animated cartoon is a series of drawings. Each drawing takes

Walt Disney also made movies using live actors. Sometimes—as in *Mary Poppins*—he made movies with both live actors and animation. He made

up one frame of film. Each drawing changes slightly from one frame to the next. When the film is run through a projector, the objects in the drawing seem to move. Animated films were first produced in the early 1900s. After Walt Disney introduced Mickey Mouse in 1928, Disney became the most famous producer of animated films in the world.

California's Disneyland Theme Park, with the Mad
Tea Party attraction (foreground) and the Matterhorn
(background), was one of Walt Disney's dreams.

nature films, realistic films, and films based on favorite books.

Walt Disney's ideas for entertaining people went beyond the movies. He was also a pioneer in creating television shows such as "Disneyland" and "Walt Disney's Wonderful World of Color."

Walt Disney dreamed of doing many things that other people said couldn't be done. Perhaps his greatest dream was to create a place where people could leave the real world behind and enter a world of fantasy and adventure. He made his dream come true when he built the Disneyland Theme Park in California.

Walt Disney spent his life exploring new ways to entertain families. He didn't pay attention when other people said his ideas were impossible. He just worked hard and followed his dreams. This is the story of how he made many of those dreams come true.

Chapter TWO

Stagestruck

This photograph of Walt Disney as a baby was taken about 1902.

Walter Elias Disney was born in Chicago, Illinois, on December 5, 1901. When Walt was four years old, his father moved the family to a farm in Marceline, Missouri.

Walt loved living on the farm. His three older brothers worked alongside their father in the fields, while Walt and his younger sister helped their mother. Eventually, two of Walt's older brothers left Marceline to start lives of their own. Then Walt's father got sick. The farm work became too much for Mr. Disney to manage. In 1910, he moved his family again, to nearby Kansas City.

Mr. Disney bought a huge newspaper route in Kansas City. His job was to deliver morning and afternoon newspapers to more than two thousand customers. Mr. Disney saw this as a family business. He expected Walt and his brother, Roy, to help.

So every day at 3:30 A.M., Walt rolled out of bed to begin a two-hour paper route. Then he went off to a full day of school, followed by another two hours of newspaper delivering in the afternoon.

Life wasn't all hard work. Walt and a friend wrote skits (short plays) in their spare time and competed in amateur theater contests. Walt also gave dramatic readings in school and delighted his classmates with cartoon drawings.

In 1917, the Disney family moved back to Chicago. By then, Walt was in high school. He was also studying at the Art Institute of Chicago and polishing his skills as a cartoonist. Mainly, though, Walt's thoughts

World War I

World War I was fought between 1914 and 1918. Almost all of the countries in Europe, plus the United States, were fighting. More than ten million people were killed during this terrible war.

American soldiers prepare for their departure to Europe to fight in World War I.

were across the Atlantic Ocean. World War I was being fought in Europe, and Walt wanted to be part of the action.

Although Walt was too young to fight, he lied about his age and joined an ambulance unit just as the war was ending. He was shipped to France as a truck driver. Walt covered his truck with cartoon drawings!

In this photograph, taken about 1918, Walt Disney stands beside his ambulance, which bears one of his cartoon drawings.

Chapter THREE

"A Good, Hard Failure"

After the war, Walt Disney moved back to Kansas City, Missouri. He was determined to succeed as an artist. His first job was drawing ads for a farm equipment catalog. Then he went into business for himself, still drawing ads. Next came a job with the Kansas City Film Ad Company. It was there that Walt got his first taste of drawing animated, or moving, cartoons.

Animation was new in 1919. Walt liked the idea of animated cartoons. But he didn't like the way they were being made. The movements were too stiff and jerky. The actions were too simple and repetitive.

Walt thought he could do better. He read books about this new art form. He studied the cartoons of other animators. When he had enough money, he bought his own motion picture camera.

This early animated cartoon was drawn by Walt Disney in 1922.

Every night after work, he used his camera to experiment with different techniques.

Soon Walt was ready to start his own animation company. He and a friend founded Laugh-O-gram Films in 1922. Walt was just twenty years old.

With Laugh-O-gram, Walt made short cartoons about people and places in Kansas City. His favorite project was a series called *Alice's Comedies*. It was to be about a real little girl who entered a cartoon world.

Walt (left) and his brother Roy with Walt's motion picture camera

But before Walt could finish *Alice's Comedies*, his company went out of business. As hard as he had worked, he couldn't make enough money to support himself. "I'd failed," Walt would later say. "But I learned a lot out of that. I think it's important to have a good, hard failure when you're young."

Walt Disney wasn't discouraged by his failure with Laugh-O-gram. He decided that the real action in animation was in the film capital of the world—Hollywoodland, California. (The name was later shortened to Hollywood.) In 1923, Walt sold his camera and headed west.

The giant letters of the "Hollywoodland" sign tower over the hills above the community.

Hollywood

Hollywood, California, is part of the huge city of Los Angeles. Until 1911, Hollywood was mostly a farming community. All that changed when the first movie studio opened in Hollywood in 1911. Early moviemakers liked Hollywood for many reasons. The weather was usually warm and dry. Movies could be made outdoors all year round in a variety of natural settings—mountains, valleys, deserts, and oceans. Today, about 225,000 people call Hollywood home. Many of them work in the film industry. They help to make Hollywood the movie capital of the world.

Chapter FOUR

Off to Hollywood

One of the first things Walt Disney did in California was talk his brother Roy into going into business with him. The Disney brothers started their film company in 1923 and worked together for the rest of their lives. They were a good pair. Walt had the good ideas, and Roy found ways to pay for them.

In Hollywood, Walt was able to continue working on *Alice's Comedies*. He also made a series of cartoons starring a character called Oswald the Lucky Rabbit. Oswald was a very popular rabbit. But he was not very lucky for Walt Disney.

Business partners Roy and Walt Disney gather oranges in a California orange grove.

Walt hired Universal Pictures, a company in New York City, to help him sell Oswald to movie theaters. But Walt made a mistake when he signed the contract with Universal Pictures. Walt had invented Oswald. But according to the contract, Walt didn't own him. Oswald belonged to Universal Pictures. As a result, Universal Pictures made a lot of money from the sale of Oswald, but Walt didn't.

Walt learned a hard lesson with Oswald. For the rest of his life, he made sure that the Disney brothers owned every cartoon and every movie they ever produced.

In 1928, Walt Disney made history when he created a cartoon character named Mickey Mouse. Mickey's first two cartoons, "Plane Crazy" and "The Gallopin' Gaucho," didn't cause much of a stir. But when Walt added synchronized sound to the third Mickey cartoon, "Steamboat Willie" became an instant hit.

Synchronized Sound

Before 1927, all movies were silent. Any words spoken by the characters were printed on the film for the audience to read. Sometimes theaters hired piano players to play music at sad or exciting times during a film. By 1927, filmmakers were learning how to produce sound as well as pictures on film. They called this process "synchronized sound" because it happened at the same time as the action. "Steamboat Willie" was the first cartoon to use synchronized sound.

This famous drawing illustrates Mickey Mouse's first appearance as "Steamboat Willie." Audiences saw the cartoon for the first time in a New York theater on November 18, 1928.

Walt Disney wanted "Steamboat Willie" to be perfect. He wanted every sound to match every action exactly. Walt hired an orchestra for the music. He hired actors and special equipment to make toots and whistles and other special effects. And when it was time to make Mickey Mouse talk, Walt used his own voice!

This 1951 illustration by Walt Disney introduces Pluto, one of Mickey Mouse's many friends.

There was no stopping Disney after "Steamboat Willie." He made more Mickey Mouse cartoons. He added other characters—Minnie Mouse (who appeared in all three previous cartoons), Goofy, Pluto, and Donald Duck. Audiences everywhere loved Walt Disney's cartoon characters.

In 1932, Disney tried something new. So far all of his cartoons had been made using black-and-white film. Now he wanted to experiment with color film. His film, *Flowers and Trees,* was the first full-color cartoon ever made. It was an instant success—and it won an Academy Award® for Best Cartoon.

The Academy Awards®

The Academy Award® statue, nicknamed Oscar

The Academy Awards®, or Oscars, are presented every spring for the best movies made during the previous year. Oscars are given for all kinds of achievements in filmmaking—for best movie, best actors and actresses, best special effects, and more. *Flowers and Trees* won Disney Studios its first Oscar. By 1999, Disney Studios had won seventy-six Academy Awards®. Of these, Walt Disney himself won thirty-two, more than anyone else has ever received.

Shirley Temple, who was then the most famous child star in the world, presents Walt Disney with his Academy Award® for *Snow White and the Seven Dwarfs*. It includes seven little Oscars for the Seven Dwarfs.

By 1937, Disney was ready for another experiment. He was tired of making short cartoons. He wanted to make a full-length animated film of the fairy tale, *Snow White and the Seven Dwarfs*. People in Hollywood didn't believe audiences would pay to see such a long cartoon. Walt's brother Roy worried that they would never have enough money to finish the film. But Walt showed them all. *Snow White and the Seven Dwarfs* made more money than any other movie in Hollywood. It won a special Academy Award® in 1939—including seven tiny Oscars for the Seven Dwarfs!

The Seven Dwarfs

Can you name all seven of Snow White's Seven Dwarfs? They are: Doc, Sleepy, Happy, Grumpy, Sneezy, Bashful, and Dopey. Other names that were considered and rejected include: Shifty, Nifty, Woeful, Soulful, Flabby, Crabby, and Awful!

Disney Studios
made *Pinocchio*
(above) in 1940.
Bambi (right)
followed in 1942.

Chapter FIVE

New Challenges

The next few years were busy ones for Walt Disney. His studio made new full-length animated movies—*Pinocchio*, *Fantasia*, and *Bambi*. By then, Disney was not drawing any of the cartoons himself. He and Roy had hired a large staff of artists to animate the movies that Walt dreamed up. Soon they needed a new studio for these talented artists.

The new Disney Studio in Burbank, California, had everything an animator could want. It had modern filmmaking equipment. It had comfortable offices with air-conditioning. It had a gym and a restaurant and parklike grounds.

Walt Disney wanted his animators—and his movies—to be the best in the world. He demanded that his staff work long hours. He paid extra money for especially good work. He even hired art teachers so his artists could keep on learning.

To make *Bambi* as realistic as possible, Disney artists took field trips to forests and attended classes that taught how animals' bodies work. Here they study the movements of a live deer in the Disney Studios.

And through it all, Disney worked right alongside his staff.

Most of Walt Disney's artists loved their work. But some of them thought Disney was too demanding and didn't pay them enough money. They said it wasn't fair that they should do the work, while Walt Disney got the credit.

The criticism surprised and hurt Disney. He knew he drove his staff hard. But he drove himself even harder. And the working conditions at his studio were as good as—or better than—those at other studios. Disney recognized that many people worked hard on each Disney movie. But audiences could never remember the names of all those people. They could remember the name "Walt Disney." Every time audiences saw his name, they knew what kind of good movie to expect.

Disney contend to work hard. During World War II, his studio made war films. Donald Duck, the Seven Dwarfs, and other Disney characters all helped support the war effort. Donald Duck was an especially big hit. When Donald told audiences to do their best to win the war, they did!

Donald Duck
wearing the
cap of an
American
World War II
serviceman

World War II

World War II was fought from 1939 until 1945. Fighting took place in nearly all parts of the world, from Europe to Africa to Asia. More than seventeen million soldiers were killed. Many more civilians—men, women, and children—also died.

Chapter SIX

Disneyland and Beyond

After World War II, Disney started his animators on three new full-length cartoons—*Cinderella, Alice in Wonderland,* and *Peter Pan.* He also started making live-action films. Exciting movies such as *Treasure Island* and *20,000 Leagues Under the Sea* pleased audiences everywhere.

Disney also began experimenting with a new kind of movie. He knew how much audiences enjoyed his cartoon animals. He thought they would also enjoy movies about real animals. In 1948, he made a half-hour movie called *Seal Island.* It was about the true-life adventures of a herd of Alaskan seals.

By the late 1940s, Disney's characters were so successful that they appeared in advertisements and on everyday products. Here, a Mickey Mouse doll sits among small boxes of Post Toasties cereal, which carried cut-outs of Disney characters on every package.

Many people thought this new movie would fail. They didn't think audiences would care about a bunch of wild seals. But Disney knew better. *Seal Island* was a huge success. It even won an Academy Award®! Audiences everywhere asked for more movies about animals—and "Disney's True-Life Adventure Films" were born.

Disney was glad audiences liked his movies. But in the early 1950s, he had an idea for an even bigger way to entertain people. Disney loved taking his daughters Sharon and Diane to amusement parks.

34

Now he wanted to build his own amusement park. Disney's park would be different from all the others. Every inch of it would be sparkly clean. It would be fun for both children and adults. It would be run by cheerful, smiling, polite people. It would be filled with wonder and adventure and magic. And it would be called Disneyland!

Walt Disney and his two daughters, Sharon (left) and Diane, in the backyard of their California home

Once again, people said Walt Disney was crazy. His brother Roy refused to give him any money for the new project. So Disney used all of his life savings. He convinced friends to loan him money. When this still wasn't enough, Disney had another great idea. He would let television pay for Disneyland!

Photos like this one, which showed families enjoying their television, helped make the new invention instantly popular.

Television

Television was still a fairly new invention in the 1950s. The first television was invented in 1929, but it wasn't until 1946 that the TV boom began in the United States. Many filmmakers were afraid of television. They thought it would keep audiences out of movie theaters. Walt Disney felt differently. Television gave him a chance to go right into people's homes and let them know all about his new ideas. "Instead of considering television a rival, when I saw it, I said, 'I can use that.'" Eventually, Walt Disney's company produced more than one hundred television series.

On October 27, 1954, a television show called "Disneyland" went on the air. Disney used his old movies and cartoons to fill up this one-hour weekly program. A year later, he started another television show called "The Mickey Mouse Club." In exchange, the American Broadcasting Company (ABC) gave Disney money to help build his dream park.

"The Mickey Mouse Club"

"The Mickey Mouse Club" was one of the most popular children's television shows ever. It featured twenty-four talented young people called the Mouseketeers. The Mouseketeers sang, danced, and performed skits. They also introduced guest stars and short films on their hour-long television show.

In this 1955 photograph, Walt Disney shows drawings of the attractions in his planned theme park, Disneyland.

By now, even Roy was excited about Disneyland. He did all he could to help make his brother's dream come true. For two years, Walt Disney worked non-stop on his new creation. When Disneyland Park opened in Anaheim, California, on July 17, 1955, it was an immediate success.

Visitors entering Disneyland followed Main Street, U.S.A. to the center of the park, where

Children and adults run into Sleeping Beauty Castle on Disneyland's Opening Day, July 17, 1955.

Sleeping Beauty Castle lay. From there, they could visit Fantasyland, Adventureland, Frontierland, and Tomorrowland. Disneyland truly was a magical place for families to visit.

Walt Disney never stopped improving Disneyland. "The way I see it," he said, "Disneyland will never be finished. It's something we can keep developing and adding to. I've always wanted to work on something that keeps growing. We've got that in Disneyland."

Soon even Disneyland wasn't enough. Disney began plans to build a second theme park in Florida. Besides having an amusement park, this one would also include Walt Disney's newest dream. He wanted to

Epcot

Originally, Walt Disney wanted to build a real city of the future, where twenty thousand people would live and work in an ideal community. This city would be called Epcot (Experimental Prototype Community of Tomorrow).

Spaceship Earth at Epcot in the Walt Disney World Resort

Eventually the plans for Epcot changed. Today, it is more like a world's fair that combines education and entertainment.

A view down Main Street, U.S.A. in the Magic Kingdom at the Walt Disney World Resort near Orlando, Florida

actually change the way people lived. So he designed a city of the future for his new park.

Walt Disney began planning his Florida dream world in the late 1950s. Sadly, he did not live to see it become a reality. Although few people knew it, Disney was sick with lung cancer. But he refused to stop working. It came as a shock to everyone but his closest family when Walt Disney died on December 15, 1966.

Roy Disney made sure Walt's dream did not die with him. Roy kept working on the Florida park. Just five years later, on October 1, 1971, Walt Disney World Resort opened near Orlando, Florida. Today it is the most popular vacation resort in the world.

Walt Disney spent his whole life exploring new ways to entertain people. Today, the company he started in 1923 is still doing just that. It has produced award-winning animated films such as *The Little Mermaid* and *Beauty and the Beast.* The Disney Channel on cable television provides family programming around the world. And more than one billion people have visited one of the Disney theme parks in California, Florida, Tokyo, Japan, and Paris, France. Indeed, it is hard to imagine a world without Walt Disney.

In Your Community

Walt Disney spent his life entertaining people. What do you do for entertainment in your community? Do you visit parks and playgrounds? Is there a nature center to walk through, or bike paths to ride along? Do you visit the library or children's museum or go to movies on rainy afternoons? Make a list of things you would like to do with your family. Then pick a date and go have fun!

Timeline

Walter Elias Disney is born on December 5 in Chicago, Illinois.

1901

Walt Disney founds Laugh-O-gram Films.

1918

During World War I, Walt Disney serves as an ambulance driver in France.

1922

Laugh-O-gram Films fails; Walt moves to Hollywood, California.

1923

Walt and Roy Disney found Disney Brothers Studio in October.

1923

1928

The world premiere of "Steamboat Willie" takes place on November 18.

Flowers and Trees is released on July 30; Disney wins his first Academy Award®.

1932

1937

Snow White and the Seven Dwarfs premieres on December 21; it wins an Academy Award®.

Now start to think about how you can entertain other people. Can you learn a card trick to impress your parents? How about organizing your friends to put on a play or circus for your younger brothers and sisters? Perhaps you could ask an adult to make a videotape of your performance to show in your own home "movie theater."

If you like to draw, go to the library and ask the librarian for help finding books about animation. Simple flip-books are a good way to get started—it's not too hard to make your pictures move!

Disney produces *Seal Island,* the first of the True-Life Adventure Films.

Disneyland opens in Anaheim, California, on July 17.

Walt Disney World opens near Orlando, Florida, on October 1.

The Disney Channel cable television network begins broadcasting on April 18.

1948 — **1954** — **1955** — **1966** — **1971** — **1983** — **1983** — **1992**

Disney's first television show, "Disneyland," is aired on ABC on October 27.

Walt Disney dies on December 15.

Tokyo Disneyland opens in Japan on April 15.

Disneyland Paris (originally known as Euro Disney) opens in France on April 12.

To Find Out More

Here are some additional resources to help you learn more about Walt Disney, Disneyland Theme Park, and Walt Disney World Resort:

Books

Bailey, Adrian. *Walt Disney's World of Fantasy*. Everest House, 1982.

Barrett, Katherine and Richard Greene. *The Man Behind the Magic: The Story of Walt Disney*. Viking Children's Books, 1991.

DiFranco, JoAnn. Walt Disney: *When Dreams Come True*. Dillon Press, 1985.

Ford, Barbara. *Walt Disney: A Biography*. Walker & Co., 1989.

Selden, Bernice. *The Story of Walt Disney: Maker of Magical Worlds*. Gareth Stevens, 1989.

Online Sites

Disneyland Theme Park
http://www.Disney.com/Disneyland/
This is the official website for California's Disneyland. You can explore the resort without leaving home! Visit Main Street, U.S.A., New Orleans Square, Critter Country, Tomorrowland, and more.

Epcot
http://www.home.earthlink.net/ ~p_williams/epcot.html
This award-winning site offers a complete explanation of Walt Disney's original plans for Epcot.

Walt Disney World Resort
www.disney.com
The official website for Orlando's Walt Disney World. Here you'll find information about the park, including scheduled events, answers to FAQs, and more.

Index

About the Author

Charnan Simon lives in Madison, Wisconsin, with her husband Tom and her daughters Ariel and Hana. Charnan is a former editor of *Cricket* magazine and sometimes works at a children's bookstore called Pooh Corner. Mainly, though, she enjoys reading and writing books and spending time with her family.

Charnan has been a Walt Disney fan for as long as she can remember. Her favorite Disney movie is *The Moon Spinners*, her favorite Mouseketeer is Annette Funicello, and her favorite Disney cartoon character is Donald Duck. Charnan went to the Walt Disney World Resort for the very first time while she was researching this book. She loved it—especially Epcot, Peter Pan's Flight, and NOT going on the Twilight Zone™ Tower of Terror!